What Catholics Are
Free to Believe or Not

Rev. H. G. Hughes

What Catholics Are Free to Believe or Not

SOPHIA INSTITUTE PRESS

Manchester, New Hampshire

Sophia Institute Press
Box 5284, Manchester, NH 03108
1-800-888-9344

www.SophiaInstitute.com

Sophia Institute Press® is a registered trademark of Sophia Institute.

Library of Congress Cataloging-in-Publication Data

Names: Hughes, H. G. (Henry George), 1868- author.
Title: What Catholics are free to believe or not / Rev. H.G. Hughes.
Other titles: Essentials and non-essentials of the Catholic religion
Description: Manchester, New Hampshire : Sophia Institute Press, 2016. |
  Originally published under title: Essentials and non-essentials of the
  Catholic religion : Notre Dame, Indiana : Ave Maria Press, 1906. |
  Includes bibliographical references.
Identifiers: LCCN 2016015537 | ISBN 9781622823512 (pbk. : alk. paper)
Subjects: LCSH: Catholic Church—Doctrines.
Classification: LCC BX1753 .H76 2016 | DDC 282—dc23 LC record available at https://lccn.loc.gov/2016015537

First printing

Contents

Preface vii

1. Faith and Practice 3

2. What Catholics Are Bound to Believe . . . 17

3. What Catholics Are Free
   to Believe or Not 55

4. What Catholics Are Bound to Practice . . . 87

5. What Catholics Are Free
   to Practice or Not 99

Conclusion 115

Bibliography 117

Preface

The following chapters first appeared in the pages of *The Ave Maria*. Their object is to aid in the removal of a very common misconception among those not of the household of faith — a misconception arising from a confusion of those things in belief and practice that are of obligation, and those things in regard to which Catholics are left free. Information on these points may also prove useful to some within the Church. The author of this little work unreservedly submits all that he has written to the judgment of ecclesiastical authority.

—Rev. H. G. Hughes
Shefford, England
Feast of the Presentation of Our Lady, 1906

What Catholics Are
Free to Believe or Not

1

Faith and Practice

There can be no doubt that misapprehension of what the Holy Catholic Church demands of her children in regard to faith and practice keeps a large number of persons, who are really people of goodwill, outside the true Fold of Christ. They are attracted, and often strongly attracted, by all they know or see of our holy religion. The venerable history of the Church; her beautiful liturgy and ceremonial, so well adapted to express the sublime truths that she teaches and to impress them deeply upon the minds of all; the very authority with which she delivers her message to the world, without fear or favor; the evident holiness of so many of her children, and the entire self-devotion that she can at all times command from them in the exercise of works of charity, whether on foreign missions or among the poor, in the hospital or on the field of battle—all these strongly attract to her many souls who remark that elsewhere such things are to be found either not at all or only in a very inferior degree.

Yet many remain where they are, outside the Ark of Salvation (at least as regards visible communion), because of some strange misunderstanding of what they would be expected to believe and to do if they submitted to the Church's authority. It is in the hope of helping such souls that this book is written. Let me say at the outset that nothing is further from my mind than any desire to dilute or minimize in the slightest degree the obligations of Catholics in matters of faith or practice. To do so would be not only most disloyal to the divinely appointed authority of the Church but also a very foolish and shortsighted proceeding that could produce only disastrous results.

No greater mistake can be committed than to lead people into the Church by concealing from them the obligations that they will assume by becoming Catholics. The natural effect of the inevitable discovery that they have been misled would be an indignant repudiation of such obligations as they had not understood from the first to be binding upon them. Thus the so-called converts would go to swell the ranks of indifferent or bad Catholics. Every word that the Church as the teacher of truth speaks to us, every command that as the guide of our conduct she lays upon us, is the word and command of God, who has said to her pastors: "He that heareth you, heareth me; and he that despiseth you, despiseth me" (Luke 10:16).

But there are false views among even the best educated of non-Catholics as to what the Church really does teach and command; and if these views can be rectified, the path to the Church will appear plainer to many. No better way, it seems to me, could be found to dissipate mistakes in this connection than a clear statement of the obligations of Catholics in matters of faith and practice. To give such a statement will be my endeavor in these chapters.

In discussing the essentials and nonessentials of the Catholic religion, I do not mean to imply that anything, whether connected with faith or practice, that has received the stamp of the Church's authoritative approval, is to be regarded as superfluous, useless, or even unnecessary. Everything that has received such sanction is thereby declared to be useful, good, and salutary and, it may be, sometimes even necessary under certain circumstances. But that sanction is of different grades, ranging from precept down to the mere declaration that there is nothing contrary to faith or morals in the matter in question.

Not all that the Church approves does she thereby impose as essentially necessary for salvation. Some things she strongly recommends; others she commands; others she simply declares to be free from any danger to faith and morality, leaving it to the faithful to adopt them or not according to the spiritual needs and bent of each. By "essentials," then, I mean those beliefs or practices that the Church demands from all as necessary for salvation; by "nonessentials" I mean, not anything that may be with impunity belittled, much less condemned, but simply points of belief and practice not made of strict obligation for all.

Faith and Practice

This having been said to obviate misconception, it will be well to consider first what is meant by "faith" and by "practice" and what is the relation between the two.

By "faith" we may understand either: (1) the *body of doctrines* held and taught by the Church; (2) the *mental act* of the believer by which he gives assent to them; or (3) the *virtue of faith*, which is a gift of God and resides as a habitual disposition or quality in the soul. It is with the first of these meanings that we shall be chiefly concerned; so the term "Catholic Faith" is to be understood as the body of truths authoritatively taught by the Church and imposed upon her children as to be believed. In other words, it is the subject matter of that intellectual assent that we call the *act* of faith.

By "Catholic practice" we shall understand all those religious acts that, whether authoritatively commanded or simply approved or recommended, are found to be in habitual or frequent use wherever the Church has children faithful to her teachings.

Faith and practice are intimately related. Practice, whether obligatory or optional, follows from what we believe, according to the earnestness of our belief. It is because we believe in God that we worship and obey

Him. It is because of our belief in the divine mission of the Church that we receive and act on her teachings as the oracles of God.

Belief is an act of the intellect, prompted indeed by the will and affections, so no one will be able to believe who persistently sets himself against believing; but still it is an act properly belonging to the intellectual faculty, since it is an assent to truth, and truth is grasped by the intellect.

Practice is an affair of the heart and the will directed by the belief of the mind. Holding most surely by faith great truths about Almighty God and His dealings with men, we are thereby moved to devotion and to the outward expression of that devotion in acts of obedience and voluntary practices of piety.

If faith does not thus lead to right practice, there is something wrong with our religion. The fault may lie in the holding of wrong doctrines, which either paralyze action or result in wrong action; or it may lie in the defective faith of him who holds, indeed, the truth but neglects to carry out into act the faith that is in him — his faith, "without works," is a dead faith (see James 2:20).

Correspondingly, any religious practice that does not find its justification in some religious truth, and its motive in a living faith, is equally to be condemned. Men do not act without giving themselves a reason for their actions, and a wrong act will be accounted for and justified by some false principle; while those who give themselves up to inaction will soon forget those principles that ought to issue in practice.

So it is in religious matters.

As wrong belief will produce wrong action, so a wrong practice, or no practice at all, will be sure to react harmfully upon belief. Thus religious practices cannot be neglected or divorced from sound teaching without harm to faith, any more than false doctrine can fail to issue in wrong practice.

What we are to believe and what we are to do as a consequence of our belief are therefore questions of primary importance in the affair of salvation. And as regards both, the Catholic Church is our divinely appointed and infallible guide teaching us the truths committed to her, laying upon us certain essential duties that follow from those truths as obligatory upon all, now determining the particular way in which some general precept is to be fulfilled, now guiding us by her approval or disapproval in such practices as the devout consideration of her teaching suggests to the faithful. By listening to her voice, we can be sure that our faith will not be harmed by wrong practice or our religious practices be the outcome of wrong belief.

I will in these pages put and answer the following four questions:

1. What are Catholics bound to believe?

2. What are Catholics free to believe or not?

3. What are Catholics bound to practice?

4. What are Catholics free to practice or not?

It is obvious that the reply to these questions might take the form of a complete course of dogmatic and moral theology. As, however, the object of these chapters is to present a statement, as brief as may be, of the obligations of the Catholic religion, the answer must inevitably take a more-or-less general form.

I hope, nevertheless, to be able to show that the Catholic Creed is, after all, a short one; that the believer is not required to know explicitly every decision of the Church as to every question and point of doctrine on which, in the course of centuries, she has found it necessary to pronounce; and that without knowing all this, a man can still hold, and hold in its entirety, the Faith once delivered to the saints and be as good a Catholic as the most learned theologian.

I shall hope also to make it clear that the Church has no secret and hidden doctrines proposed to the initiated only; and, finally, that not one of her children, simple or learned, is required to accept the Church's teachings blindly and unreasonably, or in any way to abdicate that sovereign faculty of reason that raises man so high above the level of all other created beings on earth.

Human versus Divine Faith

It will be necessary, as a preliminary to answering the four questions put above, to consider the nature of that intellectual act of assent or adherence to truth that we call faith — the act that we signify by the words "I believe." Unless we are clear as to what this means, the position of the Church as the teacher of divine truth cannot be rightly understood or our inquiry into Catholic faith and practice be satisfactorily conducted. The kind of misconception that it is the purpose of these chapters, if possible, to remove, arises in great measure, I think, from a misunderstanding — or, rather, from the want of a clear conception — of the nature of divine faith, of the grounds on which it rests, and of the position of the Church in regard to it.

One who knows what divine faith is, and what is its necessary subject matter, will not be kept out of the Church by imagining that belief, for instance, in the reality of certain alleged modern miracles or private revelations is made a condition of membership of the Church.

What, then, is an act of faith? In other words, what do we mean when we say "I believe"?

There is a conversational use of the phrase that makes it mean, "I *think* such and such, but I am not sure," as when a man says, "I believe I have seen you before." Clearly this does not express a true act of faith.

Again, I may say, "So-and-so, who is a great astronomer, predicts that an eclipse of the sun will take place next month, and I believe it." This expresses an act of faith in the word of a man.

What, then, is it which essentially constitutes an act of faith?

It is that I accept, on the word of one who from his qualifications of knowledge and truthfulness has authority to speak, some truth that I do not know by virtue of my own personal investigation. I believe that the eclipse will take place because my friend the astronomer, whose knowledge and veracity I have good grounds for trusting, assures me that it will. I take his word for it. This is a true act of faith in a human matter: an act of *human faith*.

Transfer this to something that is told me not by man but by God Himself, and add that the saving assent to what God reveals is made not by our own unaided intellect but under the influence of a divine and supernatural assistance, and we have an act of *divine faith*. An act of divine faith, then, is an assent given by us, with the help of God's grace, to some doctrine revealed by Him, because He, whose knowledge and veracity we know to be simply perfect, teaches us that doctrine with authority. This a Catholic expresses by the well-known formula of our catechisms: "I believe firmly whatever God has revealed, because He, who can neither deceive nor be deceived, has revealed it."

The fact that such an assent, in order to be faith of the kind that is pleasing to God and meritorious of eternal life, must depend on divine grace, is expressed in the definition of the virtue of faith commonly given: "Faith is a supernatural gift of God, which enables us to believe firmly, without doubting, all that He has revealed."

The act of divine faith, then, is taking God's word for a thing: a submission of our intellect to His—a submission that He helps us to make and that, far from being an abasement of our understanding, is its noblest perfection, since by it we are made cognizant, with the highest certainty, of divine facts utterly beyond the reach of our unaided faculties.

What, then, is the position of the Church in regard to the act of divine faith? She is simply God's messenger, who comes to us with claims to that office that are entirely unimpeachable and tells us what is the subject matter on which we are to exercise faith—tells us, that is, what God has said and what we must, in consequence, believe and do.

God might have chosen to speak directly to each individual soul. He has not done so—that is to say, He has not chosen that way as the normal and regular means of making known to mankind the truths of salvation, but has committed them to His Church. We believe her doctrines because they come from God, who speaks by her mouth. She is the intermediary through whom He makes them known to us.

From this it is clear that the Church has not an unrestricted right to impose upon us any belief whatever on any subject whatever. The terms of her commission are defined. She is the custodian and teacher, not the originator, of divine revelation. Her primary duty is to hand down unaltered the Faith delivered to her by the Apostles.

It is true also that her office of infallible custodian and protector of the Faith requires that she shall be able, when occasion arises, to define infallibly other truths connected with, or necessary to, the defense and safeguarding of revealed doctrine; and when she does so, she is entirely within her province.

The consideration of this class of definitions will, however, find its place in another chapter; so that for the present it is sufficient to insist on the Church's position as God's messenger, bringing to us the doctrines she has received from Him — doctrines that we unhesitatingly and firmly accept.

2

What Catholics Are
Bound to Believe

Catholics are bound to believe whatever God has revealed and the Church proposes to them as to be believed. That a man is strictly obliged to assent to anything that he is convinced has been revealed by Almighty God need not be said; it needs no proof for those who believe that there is a God and that He has made a revelation to men. As we have already seen, the Church stands to Catholics in the relation of a divinely appointed ambassador, bringing to them from God the words of eternal life. It is because we are certain of this fact that we say in our Act of Faith: "I believe whatever God has revealed *and the Church proposes to my belief.*"

What Catholics Are Free to Believe or Not

Kinds of Catholic Beliefs

Let us inquire, then, how the Church exercises her office of ambassador from God: how she delivers her message. She speaks to us in several ways and proposes to us for acceptance different kinds of truths. First and foremost, and as her chief duty, she makes known to us truths that have been revealed by God. This she does: (1) by solemnly defining truths as divinely revealed; (2) by her unanimous teaching of divinely revealed truths through the voice of her united pastorate throughout the world in conjunction with the Apostolic See; and (3) by delivering to us the Holy Scriptures with the declaration that they are the written Word of God.

Truths Proclaimed by Solemn Definitions

All these modes of teaching are of equal authority, but it is worthy of notice that her unanimous teaching (the method mentioned in the second place) is *prior in time* to the others and is also the *normal* and *ordinary* way in which the Church teaches her children.

Before a line of the New Testament had been written, and years before she thought of making a solemn definition,[1] the Church had spread the gospel over the world by means of the daily teaching of her pastors — by her *ordinary Magisterium*, as it is called.

There are to be found Catholics, even, who forget this important fact and are inclined to restrict their obligations to believing only those truths that have been solemnly defined; being under the misapprehension that solemn definitions are the normal and ordinary mode in which the Church teaches truth. This is, in the literal sense of the word, preposterous. It is putting the cart before the horse.

---

[1] The decision of the Apostles at Jerusalem on the question of the binding force of the Jewish Law on converts was, it is true, a solemn definition; but, occurring in apostolic times and being promulgated by the Apostles themselves, it is not reckoned among those definitions that the Church has put forth in virtue of her office as teacher and custodian of the Deposit of Faith delivered to her by the Apostles. The truth taught by that decree is part of the Deposit of Faith.

What Catholics Are Free to Believe or Not

As the Apostles, as soon as they had received the Holy Spirit, began to exercise at once their infallible power of daily oral teaching, so has the Church done ever since, and so will she do to the end of time. Solemn definitions are called for only on special occasions and under extraordinary circumstances; and if we had to wait for them in order to learn our religion, things would be at a standstill.

The Holy Spirit, dwelling in the Church, confers upon her the gift of infallibility, in her universal preaching and belief; so that it is impossible either for her pastorate — that is, the bishops as a body in union with their head, the Roman Pontiff — to teach false doctrine or for the faithful as a body, united to their pastors under the same supreme head, to err in belief.

In concluding this part of the present chapter I should add that the name Catholic Faith, or more fully, Divine Catholic Faith, is properly restricted to the act of assent to truths revealed by God *and* promulgated authoritatively by the Church. So also, in the other sense of the word, the Catholic Faith is the body of truths thus taught. Thus the [First] Vatican Council declares that "all those things are to be believed with divine and Catholic faith which are contained in the Word of God, whether written (Scripture) or handed down (Tradition), and proposed by the Church either by her solemn judgment or her ordinary and universal magisterium to be believed as divinely revealed."[2]

Truths defined but not as divinely revealed

We have now to consider another class of truths *taught by the Church but not proposed to us as divinely revealed.* That the Church is infallible in such teaching is one of those truths taught by her ordinary Magisterium, as is clear from her constant and universal practice. We have seen that she is not only the *teacher* but also the *custodian* of the deposit of revelation. It is her office, therefore, to protect and keep intact the body of revealed truth. Now, it constantly happens that men put forth, on a multitude of subjects, opinions that are incompatible with some acknowledged truth of

---

[2] First Vatican Council, chap. 3, par. 8, quoted in Norman P. Tanner, *Decrees of the Ecumenical Councils*, 2 vols. (London: Sheed and Ward, 1990).

revelation. In such a case the Church has the power to condemn the false opinion or to define what is the truth of the matter, even if that truth is not contained in the original revelation delivered to her by the Apostles. Without this power she could not fulfill that most important duty of "keeping the Faith"—defending and protecting the deposit of revelation.

When, therefore, the Church does define a truth, not as revealed but as necessary to the defense of revealed truth; when, too, she proscribes some error incompatible with revealed doctrine, Catholics are bound to assent to her judgment, to accept the truth and reject the error.

Some theologians, indeed, hold that every truth thus defined is, in fact, contained in the original deposit of faith, inasmuch as such truths come under the revealed general proposition that whatever the Church defines is infallibly true. It seems preferable, however, to consider with others of equal authority that such truths are not strictly revealed. As to the Church's infallibility in this class of definition, there is no question among Catholics. The latter theologians speak of the act of assent to such decisions as an act not of divine but of *ecclesiastical faith*, since we assent to them directly on the authority of the Church, indirectly only on the authority of God, who has included in her teaching office the power of infallibly pronouncing such definitions. Apart, then, from a technical discussion that is not of practical importance, it is the teaching of the Church that Catholics are bound to accept any definition of truth and any condemnation of error that she puts forth in virtue of her position as custodian and defender of revelation.

This is in no way contradictory to the statement I have made above, that the terms of the Church's commission are defined; that she has not carte blanche to define anything whatever on any and every subject. *It is only when an opinion or statement comes into contact with revealed dogma,* as opposed to it, or necessarily following from it, or so bound up with it that the revealed dogma and the nonrevealed truth must stand or fall together: then, and then only, does it come within the province of the Church to pronounce for or against it.

Her concern is with revealed truth: she is not a teacher of science or human philosophy, but she knows her own truths in all their bearings; and she knows, too, that truth cannot contradict truth; so when a scientist puts forward some theory that is *plainly* contradictory to revelation, or that denies some truth of the natural order without which revelation could not stand, she has every right, *as the keeper of the faith*, to lift up her voice.

The following extracts from the solemn definitions of the Vatican Council will at once illustrate what has been said, and show, in the authoritative words of the Church herself, what are the duties of Catholics in regard to her pronouncements:

> Wherefore, by divine and Catholic faith all those things are to be believed which are contained in the word of God as found in Scripture and tradition, and which are proposed by the Church as matters to be believed as divinely revealed, whether by her solemn judgment or in her ordinary and universal magisterium.[3]

---

[3] Tanner, *Decrees of the Ecumenical Councils*, chap. 3, par. 8.

Furthermore, the Church which, together with its apostolic office of teaching, has received the charge of preserving the deposit of faith, has by divine appointment the right and duty of condemning what wrongly passes for knowledge, lest anyone be led astray by philosophy and empty deceit.

Hence all faithful Christians are forbidden to defend as the legitimate conclusions of science those opinions which are known to be contrary to the doctrine of faith, particularly if they have been condemned by the Church; and furthermore they are absolutely bound to hold them to be errors which wear the deceptive appearance of truth.[4]

For the doctrine of the faith which God has revealed is put forward not as some philosophical discovery capable of being perfected by human intelligence, but as a divine deposit committed to the spouse of Christ to be faithfully protected and infallibly promulgated.

[4] Ibid., chap. 4, pars. 8-9.

Hence, too, that meaning of the sacred dogmas is ever to be maintained which has once been declared by Holy Mother Church, and there must never be any abandonment of this sense under the pretext or in the name of a more profound understanding. "[5]

I may add also the words of the English bishops in their joint pastoral letter of December 1899, approved by a special letter of his late Holiness Pope Leo XIII:

It may be well to insist, with the same [Vatican] Council, on the further truth — namely, that Catholics are bound to give their assent also to the decisions of the Church concerning matters appertaining to or affecting revelation, though these matters be not found, strictly speaking, within the deposit of faith. Such matters are, for instance, the interpretation of Scripture; the canonization of saints; the matter and form of sacraments in a given case, in which a dogmatic fact is under consideration;

[5] Ibid., pars. 13-14.

other facts which are called dogmatic; and the condemnation of false doctrines by the Holy See.[6]

Pronouncements by ordinary Church authority

Having now inquired into the obligations of Catholics in regard to infallible pronouncements of the Church, there remains to be considered a third class of authoritative decisions that also have a binding force upon the faithful. The Church does not in all her pronouncements intend to exercise in full her supreme prerogative of infallibility. The reason for this we may suppose to be a merciful regard for human weakness and a desire to give erring souls every opportunity of retraction before the final definitive sentence goes forth which would cast them out of the fold if they remained obdurate. Hence she frequently utters, in the exercise of her authority to teach and govern Christ's flock, words of warning, exhortation,

[6] "The Church and Liberal Catholicism: Pastoral of the English Bishops," *Messenger of the Sacred Heart* (1901): 183.

or direction, in virtue not of her infallibility, but of her ordinary ecclesiastical authority.

When she thus speaks, it is without doubt the duty of Catholics to listen and to submit their judgment to that of their pastors. This assent is one of *religious obedience* rather than of faith, though. It does pertain, in a certain degree, to the latter virtue.

If a man wishes to exercise perfectly the virtue of temperance, he must not only avoid downright excess but must put a general restraint on himself in regard to all things that might endanger temperance. So, too, a Catholic, in order to keep thoroughly sound and whole the virtue of faith that God has given him, must not be content with avoiding out-and-out heresy but must be prepared to steer clear of everything that approaches in the slightest degree thereto. It is to direct us in avoiding such things that the Church speaks from time to time warning words that, although they are not in the nature of infallible pronouncements, demand, nevertheless, our ready attention and complete acceptance.

Speaking of this assent, the English bishops in the important pastoral already referred to, say:

The second kind of assent is that elicited by virtue of "religious obedience." It is given to that teaching of the Church which does not fall under the head of revealed truth nor even under the endowment of her infallibility, but under the exercise of her ordinary authority to feed, teach, and govern the flock of Christ. To think as the Church thinks, to be of one mind with her, to obey her voice, is not a matter of duty in those cases only in which the subject-matter is one of divine revelation or is connected therewith. It is an obligation also whenever the subject-matter of the Church's teaching falls within the range of her authority. And that range, as we have said, comprises all that is necessary for feeding, teaching, and governing the flock. Under this ordinary authority ... come the pastoral letters of bishops, diocesan and provincial decrees, and (though standing respectively on higher ground, as being of a superior order and covering the whole Church), many acts of the Supreme Pontiff, and all the decisions of the Roman Congregations. It is by virtue of ordinary ecclesiastical authority, not of infallibility, that the larger number of the hortative, directive, and preceptive acts of the Church are issued.

As points of discipline may be decreed at one time and modified or set aside at another, so may novel theories and opinions, advanced even by learned men, be at one time censured by the Roman Congregations and at a later time tolerated and even accepted. For instance, the Holy Office in a case of a disputed text of Scripture or any similar point, after careful consideration — customary in matters of this importance — may declare that the arguments brought forward do not warrant the conclusion claimed for them by certain students. Such a decision is not immutable, and does not prevent Catholic students continuing their research, and respectfully laying before the Holy See any fresh or more convincing arguments they may discover against the authority of the text. And thus it becomes possible that, in time, the tribunals of the Holy See may decide in the sense which the earlier students had suggested, but could not at first establish by satisfactory arguments as a safe conclusion. In such a case loyal Catholics should accept her decision, by virtue of "religious obedience," as the one to be followed for the present. But while they gratefully accept such guidance in a matter that concerns religion, they will be careful to distinguish between this guidance and the Church's definitions of faith.[7]

The pastoral then goes on to quote the following weighty words of Leo XIII in paragraph 24 of his 1890 encyclical *Sapientiae Christianae*:

In settling how far the limits of obedience extend, let no one imagine that the authority of the sacred pastors, and above all of the Roman Pontiff, need be obeyed only insofar as it is concerned with dogmas, the obstinate denial of which entails the guilt of heresy. Again, it is not enough even to give a frank and firm assent

---

[7] "The Church and Liberal Catholicism," 185.

to doctrines which are put forth in the ordinary and universal teaching of the Church as divinely revealed, although they have never been solemnly defined. Another point still must be reckoned amongst the duties of Christian men, and that is, they must be willing to be ruled and governed by the authority and direction of their bishops, and, in the first place of the Apostolic See.

After all, when the Church speaks, even when she does not speak with all the weight of her infallible utterance, she does invariably give us *safe guidance*; for, although the speculative truth or falsity of some matter that she treats in this particular way may be, for a time, a matter of question, there can be no question at all that a Catholic is *practically* secure in listening to the voice of those whom God has set as bishops and pastors to rule the Church.

Besides the various pronouncements of the Church of which we have treated, there is a special class of doctrinal statements known as *theological conclusions*. By a theological conclusion is signified a statement of doctrine deduced from two antecedent statements, one of which is revealed, but the other known by reason only. An instance is the statement that the Son proceeds from the Father by way of an act of the intelligence of the Father contemplating His divine essence; this divine act resulting in the procession of the Word as a Divine Person. This conclusion—namely, that the Son proceeds by way of intelligence—is deduced partly from revealed truth, partly from the teachings of reason.

As to whether such conclusions are to be believed with *divine faith*, theologians differ. If a conclusion of that kind be adopted and defined by the Church, although not promulgated as a revealed truth, it would come under those matters that must be held with *ecclesiastical faith*. Otherwise, whatever the differences among theologians as to the duty of Catholics in regard to such doctrinal statements, this much is certain, and universally held: that a Catholic who should venture upon denial of a *certain* conclusion of that kind would be convicted at least of disloyalty and of a failure to keep intact the virtue of faith, which demands that we should avoid not only downright heresy but also everything approaching unbelief.

Enough has been now said, I hope, to show in general what are the obligations of Catholics in matters of faith and in those things that pertain in any way to the doctrines of faith. And to a Catholic there is nothing burdensome in all this. He knows that the Church is his divinely given teacher and guide in all that concerns his eternal salvation; he is ready, whenever and however she speaks, to listen and to obey.

He has the same trust in her that a child has in his mother. When she speaks to him, he does not require to know, before he obeys her, precisely what grade of her authority she is acting upon. Sometimes, indeed, she does speak in strong terms, making it quite clear that any who withhold their assent will thereby make shipwreck of the faith and be cast out of the fold; but she does not always choose to speak thus, nor is it needed. A good mother will not always accompany her commands, firm though they be, with threats of punishment. So it is with the Church. She knows well that her faithful children will render willing submission to her slightest word, and she reserves the thunders of anathema for great crises that must be sharply dealt with.

No good Catholic will take advantage of this to allow himself any freedom of opinion short of down-right heresy. A Catholic knows that, short of heresy, he may yet sin gravely against the virtue of faith by failure to think and believe with the Church. And in thus assenting to the Church's teaching, he in no way abdicates his reason; for his assent is not a blind and unreasoning one. On the contrary, it is eminently reasonable. What should we say of one who, himself ignorant of science, should persistently adhere to his own notions in the face of the well-established teaching of scientific men?

There is nothing unreasonable in believing those whose claim to speak with authority we are fully convinced of and who speak on a subject especially their own. The opposite course would be the unreasonable one. The Church comes to us with proven claims to be the messenger of God, who is omniscient and the very Truth itself; moreover, God has given to her as her special and proper province all that concerns salvation. On that subject, then, she is to be heard and obeyed; and to hear and obey her is the highest reasonableness.

"But," a non-Catholic might say, "what if the Church tells me to believe something that is altogether contrary to reason?" I reply, that is impossible. She cannot: that is, she cannot ask me to assent, with the assent of faith, to anything contrary to a proven truth of reason — to a truth of science established beyond doubt. She may warn me off some theory as yet *merely* a theory, and that with good reason; but she cannot contradict a known truth.

Truth is one as God is one and is consistent with itself. In reply to this very objection the Vatican Council has uttered these pregnant words:

But although faith *is above* reason there can never be any real dissension between them; since the same God who reveals mysteries, and pours into our minds the light of faith, also gave the human soul the light of reason. But God cannot contradict Himself, nor can the truth ever contradict the truth. An appearance, indeed, of such contradiction arises chiefly from this cause: either the dogmas of faith are not understood and expounded according to the mind of the Church, or mere opinions are put forth as the pronouncements of reason.

The Church, therefore, will never ask us to believe as of faith what is absurd or clearly contradicted by reason or fact. She proposes, indeed, mysteries to a complete fathoming of which reason cannot attain; but her enemies have never been able — and never will be able — to prove that any of her dogmas are contradicted by the light of reason, which, like faith, comes from God.

Teachings That Must Be Accepted

It may now be remarked: "You have given a general answer to the question "What are Catholics bound to believe?" But what an inquirer will naturally ask is: "What is the Creed to which I am expected to subscribe? What in detail are the several articles of faith to which I shall find myself committed when I am a Catholic?"

What Catholics Are Free to Believe or Not

This is a most reasonable question and demands an answer.

I reply, then, in the first place, that when you have once grasped the truth that the Catholic Church is the one religious teacher sent by God to make known to men the full and complete revelation of the Christian religion, the perplexity you naturally feel when contemplating a possible multitude of dogmas that you may be expected to believe will to a great extent soon disappear. The fear that you may be suddenly called upon to profess some new dogma that you did not bargain for, and for which you had been totally unprepared, will disappear altogether. You will know that, being the teacher of truth, the Church can never bring forward and impose upon her children anything contradicting reason. To be the bearer of a divine message and at the same time to contradict the truth of reason is an impossibility.

There is no need, therefore, to examine singly every Catholic dogma, to look up every decision of Popes and councils since the Church began, in order to find out whether you can bring yourself to give adhesion to them. If you are certain that the Church speaks in God's name, you can rest assured also that no dogma of hers will cause you uneasiness. You know she cannot teach anything that is false; you trust her, therefore, in matters that may not as yet have come to your own knowledge or been submitted to your personal investigation.

This, then, is the fundamental question for all inquirers: "Is the Catholic Church the one authorized teacher of divine truth? Is she, as she claims to be, a messenger from God?"

Explicit and implicit beliefs

"But," you will say, "I am still perplexed about the number of articles of faith. Surely, if I am to be a good Catholic, I must know what they are and believe them all."

Yes, you must certainly believe them all; but in order to do this it is not necessary that you should know them all in detail. This may appear at first sight contradictory, but it is not so in reality. A man, out of boundless trust in a political leader, may commit himself unreservedly to his program even though at the same time he is acquainted with its main outlines only and has not a detailed knowledge of its every point. Such a one would perfectly satisfy the requirements of party loyalty; although it would, of course, be to his advantage to make himself more thoroughly acquainted with the whole contents of the program he supports. He accepts all even though he does not know all. Nevertheless, he knows enough to justify him in this course of action; and, if his trust in the capacity and wisdom of his leader is well founded, there is nothing at all foolish in such a course. It may, indeed, be the only one possible for him, on account of incapacity or lack of opportunity to gain more extensive knowledge.

Now, the greater part of Catholics are in a similar position with regard to some of the Church's dogmas, with the difference that their trust in their teacher is entirely safe: she cannot deceive them, whereas political leaders are not always worthy of the confidence reposed in them. Catholics have, to begin with, the most certain assurance that what the Church teaches is infallibly true. They have, too, and are required to have as a condition of salvation, a knowledge, greater or less according to the capacity of each, of the main points of her teaching. She herself takes care that all her children shall be well instructed in the great truths of salvation, such as the doctrines of the Blessed Trinity, the Incarnation and Redemption, the Church, the sacraments, and other articles of faith of primary importance. Moreover, by every means in her power she encourages all Catholics to enter as deeply as they can into her doctrines. She hides nothing; she reserves nothing of her authorized teaching for any special class: her catechisms, her creeds, her books of theology are open to all who are capable of studying them.

But, obviously, all have not the same capacity. There must, of necessity, be details that do not come to the knowledge of the many; intricate points of doctrine that she has had to decide in settling the disputes of the learned; old, long-forgotten errors that she has had to condemn in past days; decisions of questions having a temporary interest only. A detailed knowledge of all these is not necessary either to salvation or to the perfect integrity of the faith. When we say, "I believe in all that the Church has proposed to my belief," we thereby accept *implicitly*, as theologians say, the whole of the Church's teaching. Nevertheless, she does require of us an explicit knowledge of and belief in the great truths that concern salvation. These we must learn and study according to our gifts or they will not have that practical effect on our lives that will enable us to save our souls and for the sake of producing which they have been revealed.

There are also points of doctrine of some intricacy that it is necessary we should explicitly believe and profess as a protest and safeguard against certain great heresies by which they have at one time or another been denied. Thus, for instance, in view of modern errors, Catholic children are taught to confess their belief not merely in the Real Presence of our Blessed Lord in the Holy Eucharist, but the true mode of His presence under the name of transubstantiation; and the *Catechism of the Council of Trent* gives particular directions to parish priests to explain this dogma to their people as well as the capacity of the latter will allow. Again, the wonderful harmony of Catholic theology is such that every point of the Church's teaching, however minute, may be brought under one of the great heads of Christian doctrine, in which, indeed, they are essentially involved.

Hence, in another way, those who profess belief in the Catholic Creed hold *implicitly* — that is, *equivalently* — every further doctrine that can be legitimately derived therefrom. The body of Christian truth is not a collection of miscellaneous and unconnected dicta upon faith and morals. It is a structure of marvelous unity, part dependent on part, so that he who denies one dogma makes shipwreck of the whole faith. Hence it is that the Church is able to sum up with admirable conciseness in her creeds the whole of Christian truth. Hence also it is that her longer creeds — and the longest is by no means interminable — are but fuller expositions of the ancient Apostles' Creed familiar to every Catholic child.

The Church's official creeds and catechisms

To find out, then, what a Catholic is bound to believe, it is sufficient to go to the authorized statement of the teaching of the Church as found in her creeds and catechisms. Therein is to be seen, in explicit terms, all that she demands as a condition of entering her fold. How much it is to be regretted that inquirers do not always take this simple course, which would satisfy them once for all that they will not be called upon to accept, as dogmas of faith, pious legends, or traditions that are in reality not connected with faith at all! In those creeds is to be found the deposit of faith that the Church herself can never add to or take from; there are to be seen the terms of her divine commission as the teacher of truth. And anyone who feels that he can accept what is there laid down need have no fear that anything unexpected will be suddenly sprung upon him.

For, be it observed, the Church can never impose a new doctrine as to be believed with divine faith. In the solemn definition of any doctrine — as, for instance, that of the Immaculate Conception or of the infallibility of the Roman Pontiff in his ex cathedra utterances — she says nothing new. It is beyond her power to teach any new doctrine.

What she does is simply to declare, in cases where, for some reason or another, doubt has arisen, what has been her teaching from the beginning — what, in short, was delivered to her as the truth by the Apostles of her Lord. She may, indeed, and she does from time to time, state old doctrines in clearer, more explicit, and more definite language than she had used before, making clear some aspect of truth that perhaps had been for a time more or less obscured; but she adds nothing to the substance of the revelation once made, the deposit of which contains in the germ all that can ever be made an article of faith to the end of time.

It is true that, while any revealed truth is in that condition of temporary obscurity, and until the Church has dispelled the clouds by her infallible definition, such a truth is not binding upon all. That is to say, it is not a dogma of faith; whereas after the definition, it becomes a dogma of faith.

But this is not teaching anything new: it is merely the declaration of a truth already possessed, and its presentation under a higher sanction than it had before. Any defined dogma has been from the beginning true, even if either the Christian consciousness — in other words, the mind of the Church — has not hitherto recognized it with such clearness as to impose it upon all or, having been once held more clearly, it has fallen into obscurity.

The infallibility of the Church may be explained as the power to look into her own mind and to recognize there and draw thence the sacred truths delivered to her by the Apostles. Hence comes that continuous development of doctrine that is a characteristic of the Church as a living organic body.

> The Church [say the English bishops in the pastoral letter already quoted] is continuous and indefectible in her existence and constitution; so also in her doctrine. But her continuity and indefectibility is that of a living organic being, animated by the Holy Ghost. It is not the changeless continuity of the dead letter of a book, or the indefectibility of a lifeless statue.
>
> Living beings are never stationary: they grow, while they maintain their identity. The Church also grows. She has a progress, an evolution of her own. Not only do the faithful grow in the faith, but faith itself may be said to grow, as a child grows in its own form and character, or as a tree in its own unmistakable properties. Such development implies no essential change. (Essential change is not development, progress or

evolution, but the destruction of what was, and substitution for it of something else.)

As St. Vincent of Lérins (d. ca. 445) wrote fifteen centuries ago: "It is the property of progress that a thing be developed in itself: it is the property of change that a thing be altered from what it was into something else." It was thus that this Father of the Church in the fifth century understood the unity of doctrine that constitutes the internal and substantial continuity of the Church—a unity always fixed and determinate in its principles, and in harmony with its original in the deposit of truth; but, at the same time, progressive in the inferences, definitions, and applications to which the original doctrine is rightly and logically extended.[8]

Again the pastoral quotes the same Father to the following effect:

The Church of Christ, being a vigilant and careful guardian of the doctrines committed to her,

[8] The Church and Liberal Catholicism," 188-189.

makes no change in these at any time — subtracts nothing, adds nothing, does not curtail what is essential nor add on what is not needed. She does not let slip what is her own, she does not pilfer what is another's; her whole endeavor, her one aim by the treatment, at once faithful and wise, of all questions, is to bring out into clearness what was once vague and incomplete, to strengthen and secure what is already developed and distinct, to keep watch and ward over doctrine already established and defined.[9]

Then the bishops go on to say:

Truths, therefore, at one time held implicitly, by degrees become explicitly realized and defined, as one or other of those truths becomes a more special object of attention on the part of theologians or the Holy See, in the face of existing controversies or of attacks upon her teaching from those who are hostile to her.[10]

[9] Ibid., 189.
[10] Ibid.

Not new truths, then, but truths that she has always possessed from the beginning, are the subject matter of the Church's definitions of faith. Even in the case of the second class of defined truths — those, that is, that are not, strictly speaking, revealed — there is nothing really new, nothing that was not true before. By such declarations the Church merely brings out what has been true from the beginning. For the relation of revealed doctrines to other truths not revealed has always been the same, since truth is one — and truth cannot contradict truth. Thus, although the Church may condemn today for the first time some scientific theory as incompatible with revelation,[11] it is, nevertheless, a fact that, in the nature of things, such a theory has always been thus incompatible; so that, had it chanced to be formulated in the first centuries, it would equally have been condemned, had attention been drawn to it.

Again, the Church may today define as true, and to be believed with the faith called ecclesiastical faith,

[11] I speak here of pronouncements in which the Church exercises her prerogative of infallibility.

some philosophical truth, the denial of which would involve the repudiation of a revealed dogma. But here again she states nothing that is in itself new. That philosophical truth that she enunciates has always been true, has always stood in the same relation to the truth of revelation with which it is connected. From the time when revelation was first made, that connection was always open to recognition; and what the Church does in defining it is to recognize and promulgate that connection that has, in fact, existed from the beginning. So, then, even in definitions of this class of truths, issued in virtue of her office as infallible custodian of the Faith, which goes together with her other office of infallible teacher, she promulgates nothing that is really new in itself—nothing that was not true from the first, even if the subject matter is something not contained in the original deposit of revelation.

One class of definition only can be said to state anything new—definitions, namely, of facts that are called *dogmatic*: as, for instance, the fact that some book, or certain expressions in a book, contain false doctrine; the fact of the reliability of this or that version of Holy Scripture; the suitability of a theological formula to express some revealed truth; the legitimate celebration of an ecumenical council, or the validity of the election of a Pope. It will be easily seen that such things come under the head of matters necessary for the due promulgation and for the conservation in all their purity of revealed doctrines, and that the Church is consequently infallible in their definition, in virtue of her office of indefectible custodian of the Faith. But such things involve directly a question of facts rather than of dogmas, so that in defining them the Church is in no way adding to the deposit of truth that she possesses.

I have already referred in this chapter to an important characteristic of revealed doctrines—that they do not stand apart: there is an intimate connection among them all. Hence comes that wonderful harmony of the system of Catholic theology that unites its interdependent parts into one consistent whole.

Hence, too, as we have seen, the Church is able, in her creeds or "symbols," to sum up the whole of her teaching under a few heads. That great Doctor of the Church, St. Thomas Aquinas (1225-1274) in his famous work the *Summa Theologica*, treats of the whole of Catholic doctrine according to a threefold division. First, he treats of God as the Author of all things; secondly, of the same God as the one Object for whom all things were made, and to the possession of whom all intelligent beings must tend, by means that the saint develops in detail; while in the third part he treats of the God-Man, who is the Way to God, through whose mediation we are reconciled to the Father, and who has given us in the Church the appointed means of grace and salvation.

So, again, the Apostles' Creed—which, as its name implies, goes back so far into the distance of history as to be with great reason ascribed, even as to its form, to the Apostles themselves—presents us, in its short, succinct articles, with a complete summary of Catholic doctrine.

Other and fuller creeds are but more fully developed statements of the doctrines therein contained. The most detailed of these is that of Pope Pius IV, issued after the conclusion of the Council of Trent, with a brief addition made after the Vatican Council. This creed is the one most frequently recited by converts when, on their reception into the Church, they make their confession of faith.

What Catholics Are Bound to Believe

I will conclude this chapter by repeating that any-one who wishes to become a Catholic may with ease find out what he has to believe. There is no ground whatever for fearing that any unexpected dogmas will be thrust upon him for acceptance after he has made his submission to the Church. The depth of his understanding of the sublime teachings of faith, insofar as our created and therefore limited intellects can penetrate them, must, of course, depend partly on his capacity and partly on the light he receives from God. That understanding will increase more and more as long as he lives, if he faithfully and reverently studies his religion; but he will never in this process discover anything that he will not see to have been involved in what he accepted when he first became a Catholic — unless either he or his instructor were guilty of great negligence during the important time of preparation. This, however, is a thing most unlikely to happen, since the Church herself guards against the danger by including in the ceremony of the re-ception of converts a profession of faith in which the Catholic doctrines are most clearly set forth.

What Catholics Are Free to Believe or Not

We have seen that Catholics are strictly obliged to give assent of one kind or another to three classes of pronouncements made by the Church:

1. doctrines that the Church teaches as truths of revelation

2. other truths that she defines in the infallible exercise of her office of protector and custodian of revealed truth

3. those words of warning and direction that, without calling into exercise her prerogative of infallibility, she frequently utters for the guidance of the faithful, either through the Supreme Pontiff himself, by the decisions of

sacred congregations, or by the voice of her pastorate

To the first class of pronouncements is due, as has been said, the assent of divine and Catholic faith; to the second, the assent of ecclesiastical faith; to the last, the assent of religious obedience — such an assent as we give when we bow to the superior judgment of one who may be expected to know better than we do and who has by his position a right to give us directions.

But beyond these matters there is a large field wherein a Catholic is completely at liberty to give or to withhold consent, according to his own judgment. The matters in which a Catholic is thus free may be conveniently classed under three heads:

1. opinions of theological schools or of individual theologians

2. pious beliefs

3. private revelations and particular alleged miracles

We will consider these in order.

The Opinions of Theologians

First, as to opinions of theologians: the very term *opinion* shows that there is here no question of any obligation to assent; for an opinion means precisely something about which we have not certainty — something probably true, perhaps very probably true, yet not certain.

The office of the theologian is not merely to lay down and defend what, by the teaching of the Church, is to be held as true without doubt: he has, besides, to illustrate the great Catholic dogmas by analogies taken from truths of reason — to show how marvelously they bear out and supplement all that reason itself teaches. He endeavors to penetrate more and more deeply into their inexhaustible significance. He strives to show that while the mysteries of faith, consisting as they do in revelations about the nature of the infinite God Himself, are therefore beyond the capacity of finite intelligence wholly to fathom, they contain nothing that is in open contradiction to the truths taught us by the same God through the light of reason. Moreover, the theologian draws probable conclusions from the teachings of faith, offers solutions of difficulties, and proposes reconciliations between those teachings of faith and dicta of science that may at first sight be in apparent opposition.

It is inevitable that in these matters, until the Church herself has spoken, there should be differences of opinion. One school of theology may consider this explanation of a difficulty to be right, while another school may hold to a different one, and another to a third. This learned Doctor may propose an interpretation of some obscure text of Holy Scripture; another may reject it. Thomists and Scotists and Augustinians may dispute concerning the best mode of reconciling the action of divine grace with the free will of man; and in all this Catholics are free to choose. Such matters are not of faith, and, unless the Church has stepped into the arena of dispute, we are left to adopt the opinion that appears to our reason to be the best grounded.

When, indeed, all schools of theology, carrying on their investigations under the eye of the Church, unanimously hold any doctrine to be a truth of revelation, we have a sure indication that this doctrine is the belief of the universal Church, since otherwise such unanimity would be impossible. We are therefore bound to believe it—not on the authority of the theologians, but because it is proposed to us by the Church as divinely revealed, and to be believed, in consequence, on the authority of God.

Moreover, supposing all schools of theological thought to hold a doctrine as certainly *true*, without, however, attributing to it the character of divine revelation, it would be rash for a Catholic to deny their teaching. But here, again, the obligation not to deny rests not upon the authority of theologians as such, but upon the fact that, under these circumstances, they do, when unanimous, represent the mind of the Catholic Church.

It should be observed, however, that to constitute this "consent of theologians" it is necessary that their consent be not only morally unanimous, but extending over a period of the Church's history long enough to constitute a constant belief. The consent of theologians merely for a period would not suffice. To quote the illustrious Cardinal Franzelin (1816-1886):

But when we have not this constant and unanimous teaching, but theologians of authority hold different views, and especially when they propose their teaching not as a fixed persuasion, but by way of opinion only, then, although their authority is not to be at once set aside as of no value, yet the fact of their discussion shows that the matter cannot be decided by their authority, but that we must decide according to the reasons brought forward, and adopt the opinion which (we speak of theological matters, not mere philosophical theories) seems most in agreement with the teachings of Scripture, the elucidations of the Fathers, and the mind and consent of the Church.[12]

A little later, quoting Melchior Canus (1509-1560), the same eminent theologian remarks: "A thing is not erroneous because it happens to be contrary to the dicta of the Thomists or the Scotists."

[12] Johannes Baptist Franzelin, *Tractatus de Divina Traditione et Scriptura* (Roma: Typographia Polyglotta, 1896), thesis 17.

PIOUS BELIEFS, RELICS, AND SHRINES

To come now to pious beliefs. Of these there are a multitude. They consist for the most part in a pious persuasion, resting on some tradition or upon some private revelation made to a saint, that certain spiritual benefits will be obtained by the devout performance of specified religious practices. I do not speak here of such things as the sacramentals of the Church, given to us by her express authority as an efficacious means of obtaining grace — these will find their proper place in these chapters when I come to treat of Catholic practices. Nor, of course, do I include among pious beliefs the faith we have in the efficacy of holy indulgences — a faith that, resting upon the infallible pronouncements of the Church, is much more than a mere belief.

Among pious beliefs a well-known instance is the persuasion that those who communicate devoutly on the first Friday of nine consecutive months in honor of the Sacred Heart of our Divine Lord will obtain the grace of final perseverance. I am aware that considerable discussion has lately arisen in some quarters concerning this belief, and concerning the best theological explanation of the famous twelfth promise made to Blessed Margaret Mary upon which it rests.[13] It is not, however, to my present purpose to enter into this question, which, as we are dealing now with matters that are not of faith, is immaterial to our subject.

Among pious beliefs are included also the other promises stated by Blessed Margaret Mary to have been made to her by our Lord in favor of those who should practice devotion to His Heart.

Another familiar instance is the widespread belief that those who die wearing the little Carmelite scapular will be saved; and, connected with this, the famous Sabbatine Indulgence, as it is called, according to which our Blessed Lady is said to deliver from

---

[13] Our Lord revealed to St. Margaret Mary Alacoque twelve promises associated with devotion to His Sacred Heart. The twelfth is as follows: "I promise you in the excessive mercy of My Heart that My all-powerful love will grant to all those who communicate on the First Friday in nine consecutive months the grace of final penitence; they shall not die in My disgrace nor without receiving their sacraments; My divine Heart shall be their safe refuge in this last moment."

purgatory, on the Saturday following their death, the souls of those who have died wearing the scapular and who have observed certain conditions during their lifetime.

Beliefs of this kind are usually connected in this way with some practice of real piety and utility; many of them have been expressly encouraged and approved by Popes; and they have without doubt been the source of many good works and consequent grace or merit. To cast ridicule therefore upon pious beliefs in general, to despise or scoff at those who hold them, could not be excused either from uncharitableness or a certain disloyalty to the Church, which approves or at least tolerates them.

But they are not matters of faith or obligation; their authenticity is a matter for historical investigation; they depend frequently on the authenticity of some alleged miracle or private revelation, matters of which I shall speak shortly; so that, in practice, while Catholics may not despise them, they are not bound to take up such things.

The Church leaves each of her children free to adopt them or not, according as they find them helpful (or the reverse) to their spiritual progress. Like all good things, they are open to abuse; and we sometimes hear of people so unreasonable as to think that the wearing of scapulars or medals, or the formal recitation of some prayer, will avail to salvation irrespective of conduct. It may well be doubted, however, whether cases of such extreme ignorance are anything but exceedingly rare, since the most elementary knowledge of Christian doctrine would suffice to disabuse any one of such an idea. A somewhat careless attitude about such things, a taking them up because they may happen to be the fashion, without any attempt to gauge their usefulness to the individual, or to extract from them the edification that a more careful and reasonable use of them would give, is probably more common, and is not free from the charge of a certain degree of superstition.

Pious beliefs are allowed and approved not as substitutes for earnest efforts to live a Christian life but as aids to that end; and the endeavor to make the substitution is an abuse.

For convenience's sake, we may also consider here the question of relics, shrines, and places that are the object of particular devotion. Our persuasion of the authenticity of these, while, strictly speaking, dependent on questions of historical fact, is often, nevertheless, due to a pious frame of mind that inclines us to look for special marks of God's presence and power in one place rather than another, and to expect that things and places in some way connected with our Lord and His saints have been used by God as the instruments and occasions of special manifestations of Divine Providence and have been the object of continued veneration on the part of Christians. Thus there is what may be described as a presumption in favor of those shrines and relics that a longstanding tradition offers to our devotion.

Apart from the tenet that sacred relics are to be venerated, which is of faith, and the belief that these certain favored spots are chosen from time to time by Almighty God as the scene of His wonders — a belief that is borne out by the constant practice of the Church — the persuasion we have of the authenticity of relics and special shrines, since it is partly due to considerations of a pious nature, may fitly be included under the present head of "pious beliefs." As I have said, history, in the last resort, must be the final judge, not of the propriety of the veneration shown to these objects of devotion — for which propriety we have the distinct word of the Church — but of their *authenticity*. History, in numerous cases, amply justifies devotion; while in other cases — such as that of Lourdes, for instance — not history so much as present-day fact attests the reasonableness of Catholic piety.

The famous shrines and relics — some of worldwide, others of local, renown — that are to be found throughout the length and breadth of the Catholic Church are many in number. Some of them, like the martyrs' tombs in Rome, date from the very beginning of Christianity; others are of quite late origin. The tomb of St. Peter on the Vatican Hill, that of St. Paul on the Ostian Way, and the relics of the True Cross are among the most ancient devotional treasures of the Church. It is piously believed by many that the Holy House of Loreto is actually that in which the great mystery of the Incarnation took place, and that it was miraculously transported to its present position by angels. It is piously believed that the Holy Stairs at Rome are the very steps of the Praetorium down which our Blessed Lord walked on His way to death;

that the Volto Santo, or veil of St. Veronica, bears the actual impress of His sacred face. The list might be indefinitely extended.

The relentless spirit of modern historical criticism is calling into question the authenticity of many long-cherished objects of devotion of this sort. Some of them will, doubtless, be discredited, while those that survive the test will have enhanced value in our eyes. But, whatever may be the outcome, one thing will be clear from what has already been said — namely, that Catholic *faith* is not concerned in these things.

How far, then, do the obligations of Catholics in regard to them extend? I reply that, while we may by no means deny the teaching of the Church that sacred relics and holy shrines are rightly made the object of veneration; while, too, we must not refuse to believe that God does from time to time choose special places in which His divine favors are conspicuously granted, we are perfectly free to judge of the authenticity of each particular instance according to the evidence that can be brought forward in its support, avoiding, of course, a spirit of carping criticism, and allowing full weight to ancient tradition, which in itself frequently constitutes strong evidence in favor of authenticity.

Such matters are not part of the divine revelation made to the Apostles and handed down by them to the Church; nor are they of such a nature as to be intimately bound up with any revealed truth, so as to come under the scope of her infallible authority as custodian of the Faith, except insofar as we must allow that she cannot err in her approval or toleration of this kind of devotion in general. Thus the great doctrine of the Incarnation stands firm whether or not the Holy House of Loreto is an authentic relic; the doctrine of the Redemption is untouched, if it be proved that the "Holy Face" is a comparatively late painting, or that the tradition about the Holy Stairs was unheard of until the fifteenth century.

Insufficiently Grounded Devotions

An objection might here be raised to the following effect. Catholics do undoubtedly make a great deal of pious beliefs. The wearing of medals and scapulars, the performance of certain set acts of devotion with a view to obtaining specified benefits, the visiting of various shrines and places of pilgrimage where some miraculous event is considered to have happened, form a great feature in their religious life, especially in Latin countries. If they had the assurance of faith in the authenticity of such things, this custom would at least be explained.

As it is, Catholics may be altogether deluded in expecting certain benefits from certain practices, and quite mistaken as to the authenticity of shrines and relics. Moreover, there would seem to be, in truth, some color for the assertion that the Church does impose these pious beliefs upon her children, since they are frequently the subject of devotional treatises, are spoken of in terms of high approbation in papal bulls, while acts of devotion of this kind are rewarded by Popes with the grant of large indulgences.

In answer to these objections, I would first reply that the approbation or toleration of the Church in all these matters means simply this: that we may be sure, upon the Church's authority, that our devotion, if rightly and reasonably exercised, is useful and salutary; or, in the case where it is plain that not downright approbation but rather a mere toleration is given, that there is no danger therein to faith or morals. It is a fact, which ought by this time to be sufficiently clear, that these devotions are not imposed on Catholics as matters of faith.

Next I would call attention to the teaching of the Church concerning the nature of the honor that is paid to relics, shrines, holy images, pictures, medals, and scapulars. This honor is that which is termed *relative* honor or worship; that is, it is directed not merely to the material object—shrine, relic, or picture—but to a *person*: the person, that is, whose shrine or relic or picture it is.

Consequently, even supposing a case where, by mistake, a Catholic were to venerate some spot or some supposed relic that had really nothing to do with the person whom he intended to honor, such an accident could in no degree depreciate the real value of his personal act of devotion. His intention is not to venerate, in itself and for itself, merely the material object concerning whose connection with the true and final object of his homage he happens to be in error; but he means to pay honor to God or to one of God's saints by the respect he shows to that which he supposes to have a special connection with the person venerated. His intention is good, and the person whom he wishes to honor is really honored by his act of devotion. Hence the fact of a shrine's being mistakenly connected in his mind with some special interposition of God or the Blessed Virgin or the saints, the fact of a relic's being erroneously ascribed to some holy servant of God, does not destroy the intrinsic value of his devotional act.

Again, supposing, for instance, the famous twelfth promise to rest upon an error, it still remains true that devotion to the Sacred Heart is theologically correct; that it is of the greatest spiritual benefit to all who practice it; that it may easily turn the scale in favor of salvation rather than damnation; and that the nine devout Communions made on the strength of it will be of a value simply inestimable, to say nothing of the fact that the good habit thus formed of communicating regularly every month will frequently be kept up. Without presuming for a moment to decide the question of the authenticity or exact theological explanation of this promise—about which the Church will speak if she sees it to be necessary—but merely supposing, for the sake of argument, that the contentions of its opponents are correct, it appears to me that the undoubted spiritual benefits to be obtained fully justify the approval that the Church has given to the practice of the Nine Fridays' Communion that has resulted from the pious belief of Catholics in the promise.

To pass off sham relics on the faithful, to "get up" a devotion to some shrine or sanctuary on false grounds, to publish false promises of spiritual or temporal benefits to be gained by some devotion — these things would indeed be most reprehensible and would meet with the sternest repression from authority; but there may be perfectly innocent mistakes about these matters, and it is to such that the foregoing remarks apply.

As to bulls of Popes published in praise of relics or places of pilgrimage whose authenticity may, in the light of historical research, become doubtful, we must remember the words of Father Thurston, S.J.:

> The approval of the Holy See which may be accorded from time to time to such popular devotions does not involve any infallible pronouncement upon a question of pure history. It

implies that reasonable care has been taken to exclude fraud or the probability of error, but that such care is necessarily proportioned to the canons of historical criticism prevalent at the period at which the approbation was first granted. Hence it may readily be allowed that the Pontiffs of the fourteenth and fifteenth centuries were often satisfied with evidence that would be far from conclusive in our own more skeptical age. Similarly, the facts which are recounted in the *Martyrologium* or the *Roman Breviary* are not guaranteed free from all error because these books are formally authorized by Papal Bulls. All the world knows that corrections and emendations are occasionally made in statements which the progress of knowledge has shown to be no longer defensible. But where the disproof of an old tradition depends only upon negative criticism, the Holy See is naturally slow to act.[14]

[14] Herbert Thurston, *The Holy Year of Jubilee: An Account of the History and Ceremonial of the Roman Jubilee* (London: Sands, 1900), 190.

What Catholics Are Free to Believe or Not

With regard to the grant of indulgences for acts of devotion performed in some place erroneously supposed to possess a sacred connection, we should remember that, although the devotion, or some particular form of devotion, doubtless grew up in the Church because of that supposed connection, yet it is the *act of devotion* that is rewarded with indulgences; and such acts of devotion need not depend on an accidental question of history. If and when it is proved conclusively that any object of veneration is not authentic, the ecclesiastical authorities will always take proper measures.

Thus the "Table of the Last Supper," preserved in St. John Lateran, was formerly the object of great devotion, being publicly exposed in the church on certain days. Now, since great doubt has been thrown upon the alleged fact of its being the identical table on which our Blessed Lord instituted the Holy Eucharist, this is no longer done.[15]

[15] Since the above was first written, it appears that the Holy Table has again been the object of public devotion; but this fact does not constitute an infallible assurance of authenticity.

Anyone who wishes may see it for the asking, but it is not brought prominently forward as before. Surely no one will say that all the fervent acts of devotion formerly paid to it—not, that is, to the material wood, as such, but to the great mystery of the Blessed Sacrament—counted for nothing in the sight of God. It is difficult to understand the spirit of those who would leave off saying the Rosary because a modern writer brings forward reasons to show that the person to whom its great utility was revealed, and who was entrusted with the task of promulgating it, was not, after all, the great St. Dominic. Surely that utility is not altered by a mistake in history.

Whether such popular shrines as the Holy Stairs or the Holy House of Loreto will ever be interfered with by authority on account of destructive historical criticism may be doubted. Such things have taken deep root in the affections of the people; they are the cause of true and real devotion; they bring home to the faithful the great truths of the Christian religion, and it would seem both unnecessary and heartless to abolish them. Of this the Church herself is the judge.

What Catholics Are Free to Believe or Not

Meanwhile Catholics are perfectly free to hold or not to hold these pious beliefs that we have been considering. They must not deny their utility to many, even if not finding them of use to themselves; they may not despise or ridicule those who do make use of them and who find them helpful to their spiritual life. Nevertheless, to repeat it once more, the Church does not impose them as matters of faith in which we are bound to believe.

SOME MIRACLES

Concerning the miracles recorded in Holy Scripture, there can, of course, be no question that Catholics are bound to believe in them. To doubt them would be to doubt the inerrancy of Holy Writ. It is not, therefore, of those that I speak now, but of miracles that have taken place since scriptural times and are often termed *ecclesiastical miracles*.

It was Cardinal Newman who said that the Church is hung about with miracles like gems; and no one who has any acquaintance with Church history can doubt that this has always been so through the long ages of the Church's life. It is so plainly part of the

Church's ordinary belief and teaching that miracles both can and do from time to time happen, that a Catholic may not deny either of these truths. But with regard to this or that particular miracle recorded in Church history or the lives of the saints, we are free to accept it or not, according as the evidence is satisfactory or otherwise. That evidence is frequently overwhelming, and such as to convince any man of sense who does not begin with the skeptic's principle that miracles are an impossibility, or with the arbitrary postulate of most Protestants that they stopped with the age of the Apostles.

Moreover, for Catholics, no inconsiderable evidence is afforded in particular cases by the very careful inquiry instituted by ecclesiastical authority. A story familiar to many of my readers is that of the English Protestant who was shown in Rome the documentary evidence in favor of certain miracles alleged to have been worked through the intercession of a deceased holy man whose cause for beatification was before the authorities. On reading the evidence the Protestant exclaimed that it would be enough to convince a Protestant British jury.

"It has not convinced us," replied the Catholics.

The strictest inquiry is made into the proofs of miracles, whether alleged to have been worked by a saint during his lifetime or obtained by his intercession after death; so that we may with full confidence accept those that have been authoritatively examined and admitted by the appointed tribunals of the Church.

Nevertheless, rash though it would be, and even disrespectful, to set up our judgment against that of authority in this matter, and foolish as it would be to reject plain evidence, particularly when it has satisfied those appointed to adjudicate upon it, the Church does not impose belief in any particular ecclesiastical miracle as a matter of faith.

In this connection it should be noticed that not miracles, but heroic virtue is the primary subject of inquiry in the process of canonizing a saint. Says Benedict XIV:

> When inquiry is instituted for the purpose of beatification or canonization, no examination is made of miracles until *after* the heroic virtues or the martyrdom of the servant of God

has been proved. These virtues are the first and most decisive witness to sanctity. Visions, prophecies, and miracles are of only secondary importance; and they are absolutely ignored if proof of heroic virtues is not forthcoming.[16]

Catholics may not, then, deny the possibility or the fact of ecclesiastical miracles in general; it would certainly be rash and disrespectful to cast doubt upon those that, after careful investigation, have been passed by authority in processes of canonization; while with regard to others we are in no way bound to accept any one in particular. They stand or fall by the evidence forthcoming in their favor.

PRIVATE REVELATIONS

To come now to the question of *private revelations*, of which we read in the lives of many saints: these, or the documents in which they are recorded, are from time to time approved by the Church. In order to understand the attitude that Catholics ought to adopt

---

[16] Quoted in Henri Joly and George Tyrrell, *The Psychology of the Saints* (London: Duckworth, 1898), 80.

toward them, we must first inquire what precisely is the nature of such approbations. On this question Cardinal Franzelin writes as follows:

> As regards the judgment of the Church, by which private revelations of this kind are sometimes approved, such judgment is not intended as proposing these revelations to the faithful as to be believed with divine faith, but as declaring (a) that there is in them nothing contrary to the Catholic Faith, nor to good morals and Christian discipline; and (b) that there is sufficient indication of their being true to justify their being piously and prudently, and without risk of superstition, believed with *human* faith, and also to justify their being read by the faithful for the purpose of edification.[17]

Lastly, he lays down that (c) after such approbation by the Church it would be wrong to *cast contempt upon them*.

[17] Franzelin, *Tractatus de Divina Traditione et Scriptura*, thesis 22.

In the matter both of approved miracles and approved private revelations, the wrong committed by a Catholic in "casting contempt" would be not a sin against divine faith, which, as the Cardinal points out, does not come into the question, but an error of imprudence and rashness in setting up our judgment against that of the tribunals appointed by the Church to inquire into these things. Their carefully considered decisions merit an assent of "human faith" which it is nothing but reasonable to accord. On the nature of private revelations Cardinal Franzelin says:

> Revelations and prophecies which since the times of the Apostles have been made, are now made, and will be made in the Church, *do not belong to the deposit of Catholic Faith* [the italics throughout are mine] entrusted to the Church to keep, to preach, and to evolve. The reason is that these revelations are not directed to the universal Church, but to private individuals. They are called *private* individuals because they are not constituted by God as His legates

to the Church, as were formerly the prophets and Apostles and holy men who were inspired to write the Sacred Scriptures; but they receive such revelations either for their own direction and benefit or for the *private* direction and benefit of others. Hence neither do they properly pertain to the *evolution* of the Catholic Faith, to carry out which Christ our Lord has instituted, with a promise of infallible direction, the ordinary ministry, consisting of the visible Head of the Church as the principle and foundation of the unity of faith, and of the apostolic succession united to that Head. Hence, according to Benedict XIV (in his work on the Canonization of Saints), amongst the reasons that render private revelations suspect is that by means of them things are said to be revealed which are still under consideration by the Church.

Private revelations, then, are not to be believed with an act of divine faith, except by those to whom they are directly made with an infallible assurance of their divine origin. Whether this infallible assurance is given even to the recipients of such revelations is a matter of discussion among theologians. These revelations, then, are to be accepted by us merely on *human faith*, meriting credence or not according to the evidence for their genuineness; in which evidence the approval of the Church in the sense just explained is an important factor. Of private revelations, says M. Joly:

A considerable number come to us on very trustworthy authority; as, for instance, those which St. Teresa relates of herself. From a purely human point of view, I know of no evidence worthy of credence on any subject, if we are to reject the great Carmelite saint's testimony, which she gives with so many precise distinctions and luminous explanations.[18]

And of all phenomena of this class, whether visions, revelations, or miracles, the same author wisely observes, after pointing out one of the tests of genuineness:

[18] Joly and Tyrrell, *The Psychology of the Saints*, 75.

At other times the character alone of the person will ensure, first of all respect, and then a reasoned acceptance of the truth of the revelation. In cases of this latter kind, we may say that it is the proved sanctity of the person which reassures men's minds as to the truth of the phenomena, rather than the phenomena themselves which gain credence, be they revelations, prophecies, visions, or any other favors. The same is true of miracles.[19]

And again:

More than anyone else, St. John of the Cross has labored to impress upon men the teaching of Catholic Tradition: that phenomena of this kind do not constitute sanctity. We may go further and say that in those countries which produce saints, and where saints are most honored, these occurrences always, in the first instance, create distrust and suspicion.[20]

[19] Ibid., 79.
[20] Ibid., 75.

These extracts, as well as what has been said above about miracles, should be enough to disabuse anyone, who is not fixed in his prejudices, of the idea that the teaching of the Catholic Church consists chiefly in a mass of incredible wonders to be without question blindly accepted by the faithful. It is strange that it should be necessary even to mention so absurd a conception of our holy religion; but it is, unfortunately, a conception that still possesses the minds of many. Real miracles and genuine visions and revelations are few and far between; and the Church herself is the first to recognize that such things are "subject to a thousand dangers, imitations, and illusions."[21] Only upon unexceptionable proof does she give any sort of approbation to them.

Because we see in foreign countries shrines literally covered over with ex-voto offerings, we are not to conclude that each of these represents a miracle examined and approved by ecclesiastical authority. Many of them are in thanksgiving for ordinary answers to prayer—for recovery from illness that may

[21] Ibid.

have been quite naturally brought about, though rightly regarded as a favor from Divine Providence, which such things certainly are. Where faith is bright and living and vivid, it is a natural consequence that the common people should not always make fine distinctions in these matters and should even sometimes see a miracle where there is not one in the strict sense. Shall we prefer the cold spirit of unbelief to a faith well grounded as to essentials, filling the lives of those who are so happy as to possess it with light and joy, although it may sometimes lead them to overpass the strict limit, always observed in authoritative teaching, that divides the supernatural from the ordinary effects of that Providence who is the source alike of nature and of grace?

4

What Catholics Are
Bound to Practice

The Catholic Church is acknowledged by her children as their infallible guide, not only in matters of belief but in conduct also. And, indeed, since belief is for the sake of conduct, and directed to conduct, we should expect that the religious society that teaches the truth should also point the way to right living.

So it is with the Catholic Church: the truths that she proclaims are saving truths, addressed not merely to the intellect but also to the heart and the will. It is one of the signs of her divine origin that she satisfies both heart and mind — confirming, developing, and completing that instinctive teaching of man's understanding and conscience that we usually speak of under the name of natural religion — the revelation of divine truth and law written on the heart of man. All truth has a value in itself and is admirable for its own sake; but religious truth has always a practical, not simply a speculative, value; and only he profits rightly by the heritage of divine revelation who strives to make it bear upon his life. It is the constant endeavor of the Church to aid us in doing this.

Hence, recognizing that true religion is a right life molded upon true beliefs, from her speculative doctrines she draws practical conclusions — that is, she instructs the understanding in order to guide the will; and in this work she is infallibly preserved from error by the spirit of her Master, who is not only the Truth, but the Way and the Life.

THE GENERAL OBLIGATION OF WORSHIP AND SERVICE

From what the Church teaches us about God, then, and about our relations to Him, there follow certain duties that we owe to Him. These are summed up in the twofold obligation of worship and service. Thus much of his duties man might have learned without a Church; but the Church, having been formed by

the Son of God to continue His work of evangeliza-
tion, tells us in His name what worship and what
service we are to render, and how. Moreover, as God's
accredited representative, she claims a service and
obedience due to herself — or, rather, due to Him in
her. Above all, preaching the doctrine of her divine
Founder, she tells us that both worship and service
are to take their rise in, and be permeated through
and through by, love of God.

Thus her primary message to mankind is: "Worship God and do His will for love of Him"; and she
provides ways and means of doing this that she has
learned from Jesus Christ and the Holy Spirit, who
dwells within her.

Vested with divinely granted authority, and guided
into all truth by the Spirit of Truth, she is able to
particularize this general precept and has power to
impose such regulations upon the consciences of
her children as she knows to be conducive to its due
observance. Hence her code of morality, and those
laws that we know as the precepts of the Church. In
these two is comprised all that Catholics are bound
to practice.

What Catholics Are Free to Believe or Not

Of the Church's code of morality it is not my intention to treat. Based on the Ten Commandments, it would be generally acknowledged as binding upon Christians by those for whom I write. Nor is it necessary here to refute oft-refuted calumnies, such as the old lie that the Church advocates the doing of evil that good may come, or teaches that a good end justifies an evil means, or that lying is allowable.

THE PRECEPTS OF THE CHURCH

I shall confine myself in this chapter to those distinctively Catholic practices that the Church enjoins as necessary to that good life lived for love of God that it is her mission to promote among men.

To take, then, first, the obligation of worship that arises from the relation of the creature to his Creator. This worship must include the four elements of adoration, thanksgiving, propitiation for sin, and prayer. The Catholic Church possesses the only form of worship on earth which fulfills these four duties in a way entirely worthy of the infinite majesty of God. That form of worship is the Holy Sacrifice of the Mass, in which for those four ends the oblation of the true Body and Blood of the Incarnate Son is offered to the Father. What wonder that the Church enjoins upon her children as a solemn obligation to participate in the offering of this sacrifice! Particularizing the natural obligation that rests upon every human being of devoting some notable part of his time to the worship of his Maker and Father, and possessing the most perfect means of fulfilling it, she commands us to observe the Sundays and certain holydays by devoutly hearing Mass; adding, for the more complete consecration of those days, a prohibition of ordinary weekday labor. This precept we know as the First Commandment of the Church.

As we have already seen, the Church's law of conduct is the law of love. He who loves will not refuse some pain and self-denial. Moreover, without self-denial and restriction the spirit cannot be free of the bondage of the flesh and fleshly desires. Men found that out before Christianity dawned upon the world. For this double reason, to train her children to the proof of their love of God by the taking up of the cross, and to aid them in subduing their carnal appetites to the spirit, she imposes upon them the duty of fasting and abstinence at certain seasons. Hence the Second Commandment of the Church: to keep the days of fasting and abstinence.

Every Catholic knows that he is not expected to injure his health by the observance of this precept, and thus to incapacitate himself from the performance of his daily duties. The duties of one's state of life, performed for God, come first and foremost in the appreciation of the Church as well as in the right order of things. Piety that does not help to this is a sham. Therefore, the Church is always ready to grant a dispensation to all who can show good cause for being relieved of the obligation of fasting or abstinence; although, at the same time, she recommends or enjoins, according to circumstances, some alternative form of self-denial that will not interfere with other duties.

The next law of the Church concerns sin and the means and conditions of forgiveness. In none of the man-made religions that have sprung up since Jesus Christ founded the Church has due proportion been observed in this matter. Error, as it always does, has rushed into one or other of two opposite extremes. While in the early days of Christianity the tendency of heretics was to exclude some sins altogether from the hope of pardon, modern religions have to a greater or lesser extent lost the sense of personal sin and of the need of reconciliation with God. The Church from the beginning has steered the middle course, which is also the true one. She excludes none from pardon, whatever his guilt, provided that he is penitent; she insists on penitence as well as upon a humble acknowledgment of personal guilt. This acknowledgment takes a form that the instincts of nature itself point out as the condition of forgiveness — a detailed confession of the sins committed; hence the Third Commandment of the Church obliging the faithful to go to confession at least once a year.

Knowing that, since the promulgation of the gospel, the prerogative of pronouncing God's forgiveness in His name has been entrusted to her by the commission of Jesus Christ Himself — "Whose sins ye shall forgive they are forgiven" (John 20:23) — she will not allow her children to deprive themselves, without strong protest on her part, of this necessary means of grace. Her children clearly understand that she makes no claim to forgive in her own name; and that although they may deceive the priest who exercises this ministry, and extort absolution from him on false pretenses, *that* judgment will not be ratified in heaven. With confession as without, repentance and purpose of amendment are necessary for forgiveness.

The motive of the next commandment of the Church is the same as that of the preceding—a desire, namely, on the part of the Church to prevent neglect of a necessary means of salvation. Mindful, therefore, of the words of Jesus, "Unless you eat the flesh of the Son of man, and drink his blood, you shall not have life in you" and "He that eateth my flesh, and drinketh my blood, hath eternal life" (cf. John 6:54-55; RSV = John 6:53-54), she lays upon us her Fourth Commandment: to receive the Blessed Sacrament at least once a year—and that at Easter or thereabouts.

The Fifth Commandment enjoins upon the faithful the duty of providing for the support of their pastors; and the sixth forbids marriage within certain degrees of kindred, and the *solemn* ceremonies of marriage in certain penitential seasons.

In the general law of worshipping God and of doing His will from the motive of love, and in these six commandments of the Church that interpret and define that law on certain points, providing thereby for its better observance, we have all that is of positive obligation for a Catholic.

By that motive — which, of course, includes love for one's neighbor, as equally with ourselves a child of the Heavenly Father, the object of His predilection, the redeemed of His Son — a man's whole life is rightly ordered in its active relations toward God and His fellowmen. By those laws he is directed to the essential means of performing God's holy will. If anyone wishes to know the Church's conception of a good Christian life, he will find it simply and excellently set forth in any catechism.

To go further into these details here would carry me beyond my scope, which is merely to remove certain misconceptions as to the strict obligations of Catholics. When we have said that the Church teaches us to worship God by faith, hope, and charity, and that the greatest of these virtues is charity — love of God, and of men for His sake — we have summed up the Catholic religion.

It remains, then, to add here only that, while providing for what we may call the minimum in

Christian practice, the Church has never ceased to put before her children the higher standard of evangelical perfection to be aimed at for love of and in imitation of the perfections of God.

To all she cries aloud the exhortation of the Sermon on the Mount: "Be you, therefore, perfect, as also your Heavenly Father is perfect" (Matt. 5:48). With what fruit she does this the lives of her saints and the holiness of many thousands of her children at all periods of her history bear ample witness.

No earnest Catholic troubles himself about the minimum that he may perform; nor would any inquirer of goodwill do so, except for the purpose of getting rid of an exaggerated notion of what would be required of him if he were to submit to the Church. As soon as he began to understand the spirit of the Catholic religion—its intrinsic beauty and reasonableness, its evident power to satisfy all the spiritual needs of the souls of men—the tried efficacy of the means it offers, whether obligatory or free, to promote the great ends of holiness and salvation would produce in him the same desire that every earnest Catholic feels: not only to use to the full such means as are essential, but also to take advantage of the additional helps that the Church offers in so great abundance to suit the particular needs of individual souls.

I have still to speak of those numerous practices of Catholic piety and devotion in regard to which we are left entirely free. If it shall be made even a little clearer to any inquirer that the Catholic religion is not to the children of the Church (as it appears to so many who are not of her) an intolerable burden, but the highest of privileges, a sweet and easy yoke, a help and not a hindrance to happiness here and hereafter, the object with which I write will have been attained.

5

What Catholics Are Free to Practice or Not

One of the most fruitful sources of misconception in regard to the Catholic religion is the general ignorance prevalent among those outside the Church as to the true meaning of what we call *devotional practices* and their place in the religious system of which they form a part. Our good non-Catholic friends observe us devoutly "telling our beads," kneeling in prayer at this or that shrine, wearing scapulars and medals, reciting certain prayers in honor of the saints, taking holy water, receiving blessed ashes, candles, or palms; and they are apt to conclude that all these things stand upon the same level as the reception of the sacraments or the observance of the moral law and the commandments of the Church.

What Catholics Are Free to Believe or Not

Not knowing the distinction between essentials and nonessentials, they class together all the practices that they observe to be in use among Catholics and think that they are all equally binding upon us. Finding some of these practices very distasteful to them, failing to see any signification or usefulness in others, they deem that they could never bring themselves to embrace them even for the sake of that peace and certainty of faith that they often instinctively feel is not to be found elsewhere than in the Catholic Church.

Devotional Practices

To remove this misunderstanding, it will be necessary to explain what is meant by Catholic *devotions* and to show what place they hold in the life of Catholics and of the Church as a body. I shall make no excuse for quoting from a recent writer who has handled this subject with admirable clearness:

There is a beauty in the theological meaning of the term "devotion" which has been lost to its ordinary, everyday sense. We should have rather to use the cumbersome word "devotedness" to express the signification of St. Thomas, and that which we have in view in the use of the word in the following essay. We will, however, retain the original term, with the proviso that readers shall understand it in the accepted theological sense, as meaning the English "devotedness" or the French *dévouement*. It is according to this meaning that we wish to contrast "devotion" with "devotions," not as things contradictory and incompatible, but as different manifestations of spiritual life, of which the latter should subserve the former, should at once spring from it and minister to it, if they are to preserve their character as legitimate products of spiritual life."[22]

Certain observances, as we have seen, are made obligatory by the Church upon all Catholics; some because, as in the case of the sacraments, they are the regular and appointed channels by which the life of

---

[22] Maude Dominica Petre, *Where Saints Have Trod: Some Studies in Asceticism* (London: Catholic Truth Society, 1903).

divine grace flows through the whole body; others because they are of peculiar and universal efficacy in ensuring a practical Christian life. But beyond these, there is the very large class of practices that go under the general name of Catholic devotions.

Not essentially necessary to the spiritual life of a Catholic, as are the sacraments, nor of such universal efficacy in the promotion of the essentials of a practical Catholic life as are the precepts of the Church, devotions are, nevertheless, of greater or lesser utility as helps to true devotion. This greater or lesser utility depends, as is pointed out in the foregoing extract, upon their source as real manifestations of healthy spiritual life — as originating in devout meditation enlightened by sound doctrine — and on their tried efficacy as instruments in the promotion of a high standard of Christian practice among those who make use of them.

Men's souls have many needs in common, yet each particular soul or class of souls has its own special needs. Catholic devotions are intended to meet these needs, both common and individual. Thus it is that we find in the Church so great a variety of devotional practices, some of a more-or-less universal character, coextensive almost with the Church herself, as satisfying wants that are felt by all or by the greater part of the faithful; while others are of less extension as appealing to certain souls only.

The attitude of the Church herself toward these devotional practices is somewhat different from her attitude in matters of faith. Of both she is, of course, the supreme judge; but, in the nature of things, her judgments in doctrinal matters must more often be strict and peremptory than in the matter of devotions. While it is true that not only will false doctrine produce wrong practice, but wrong practice will also frequently result in damage to faith, yet the boundaries within which varieties in practice may move without damage to faith are wider than those limits beyond which opinion in matters of doctrine passes into error.

The Church, therefore, is very tolerant in regard to practices of devotion The moment, however, they involve or imply a false conception of the teachings of religion, she puts her ban upon them; but, with a deep insight into human nature and its wants, she does not hesitate to permit many practices that are the outcome of a simple faith and affection and are of real use to large numbers of her children, although they may draw a smile or a jibe from superior and "enlightened" persons. Guided in this matter, as well as in her doctrinal teachings, by the Spirit of Truth promised to her in the beginning, she extends to such practices, as pious meditation on the truths of faith suggests to her children, now her strongest approbation or recommendation, now her protection or kindly toleration, according as she judges them to be of universal utility or useful for certain persons only, and according to their greater or lesser efficacy in the promotion of true holiness. Thus, as the writer whom I have already quoted puts it:

> The Church reserves to herself a certain right of discrimination in this matter. She meets the various devotions that arise with approval or toleration or condemnation, according as she judges them sound in doctrine or the reverse, and helpful or harmful or indifferent to the spiritual life. By her approval she guarantees

that they are sound in doctrine, and, at least, have it in them to be helpful to salvation and sanctification. By her toleration she ensures to them a certain negative virtue and harmlessness, without any assertion as to their being actually ennobling and useful. But here her mission ends. It is not as with the sacraments, which she presses on the use of the faithful; it is not as with her doctrinal definitions, which are to help on the life of spiritual knowledge, as the sacraments help on that of grace.

In this other field she assumes to herself no final responsibility, except in the merely negative manner which we have indicated. She approves in the name of doctrine; she permits in the name of liberty; but she commands nothing except that toleration and respect which she has herself manifested, and she refuses to take up that burden of individual responsibility which many are too ready to fling on to her shoulders at every turn of the spiritual life. The right of choice and its duties remain to the individual soul, which has to manifest its loyalty by exercising, in things religious, that temperance and courtesy which are the spiritual counterpart of social good manners. We are not bound to practice all the devotions which the Church declares holy and harmless; but we are bound to restrain our criticism in the spirit of respect for our fellow Christians; and we are also called on to conform to certain general usages under pain of becoming boors in our religious community.[23]

The Church, then, wisely leaves these things to our own choice, in which we must be guided by the adaptability of various devotions to the needs of our own souls, and the approbation extended to them by ecclesiastical authority; the latter being, in the main, protective rather than directive. She thus insures us against any practice contrary to the spirit and teachings of the Catholic religion and leaves it to ourselves to select those devotions that we find most conducive to our own progress in the spiritual life.

[23] Petre, *Where Saints Have Trod.*

Thus, far from being bound down and restricted in the development of spirituality, Catholics have the widest freedom—far more than is to be found in any of the sects among whom, just as faith has suffered by insistence on some truths to the exclusion of others, so also spirituality suffers by insistence on some particular method of devotion, with the inevitable result of cramping and confining the spiritual energies that, given free vent, would lead to higher things.

We have already noticed that devotional practices do not all stand on the same footing. There are some that experience has proved to be so generally helpful to a fuller and more fruitful Catholic life that they have obtained almost universal acceptance among the faithful and have been encouraged and promoted far and wide by the Church, who has put her seal upon them in an unmistakable manner. Such are the well-known devotion of the Rosary, the devotion to the Sacred Heart of Jesus, various practices in honor of the sacred humanity of our Divine Lord, others in commemoration of the various mysteries of His life and Passion.

Much as she encourages these devotions, however, the Church does not make them obligatory upon all.

What Catholics Are Free to Believe or Not

A Catholic, indeed, who should deny that the sacred humanity, as personally united to the Eternal Word, is to be worshipped with divine honor, or who should refuse that worship to our Lord, would make shipwreck of the faith. So also would he who would deny the utility and propriety of invoking the intercession of our Lady and the saints.

Catholic Freedom in These Matters

Nevertheless, a Catholic is not compelled to invoke the saints or to take up any special form of devotion to our Lord's sacred humanity, excepting, of course, the worship he is duty-bound to offer to Him present on our altars in the Blessed Sacrament. But he is not forced to take up the special devotion to the Sacred Heart or to the Five Wounds or to the Precious Blood. At the same time, any child of the Church who would set up his private opinion in opposition to that of the whole body would, in the words of the writer I have quoted, do so "under pain of becoming a boor in his religious community." He would, moreover, be depriving himself of a means of furtherance in the Christian life, of the efficacy of which, in view of the strong approbation of the Church, there can be no doubt.

The history of certain widespread devotions plainly shows them to have been awakened in the Church by the action of the Holy Spirit, to meet the needs of souls at various periods of the Church's life. In these matters the Church moves with the times; and not to move with her argues a certain failure to realize those teachings of faith that express themselves from time to time in new forms of devotional practice, according as fresh aspects of ancient truths exhibit themselves to her understanding.

Not unfrequently such fresh aspects are the consequence of the rise of some error that draws attention to a view of doctrine not explicitly considered before by the Church at large; and a devotional practice arising from this new contemplation of Truth, unchanging in itself, may be a protest against prevalent heretical tendencies. Such was undoubtedly the case with the devotion to the Sacred Heart, which, by its warmth of tender affection to the person of our Blessed Lord, and its lively appreciation of His love for men, together with a consequent great increase of the use of those sacraments by which we enter into the closest union with Him, acted as an antidote to the cold formalism and harsh rigorism of the Jansenist heresy.

So, then, should a Catholic abstain from a devotion of this kind, one would say of him that he is not compelled to take it up, but that he proves himself more or less out of sympathy with the spirit of the Church by refusing to follow her in that continual progress she exhibits alike in the development of her understanding of doctrine and in consequent adaptations of practice. Not to follow her in such adaptation to new needs and conditions is at least to run the risk of finding oneself out of harmony with her teaching. The appeal to antique as against contemporary ways of devotion has a dangerous kinship with the appeal from the teaching of the present living voice of the Church to the dead letter of the past.

Holy Indulgences and Sacramentals

There are two other ordinances of the Church that enter largely into Catholic life and may be, for the purposes of this chapter, conveniently classed under the head of "devotional practices," although differing in one important respect from such devotions as we have hitherto considered. These are holy indulgences and the sacramentals of the Church. They differ from other devotions in that they have a close connection with the sacraments themselves and are consequently recommended and even pressed upon the faithful by the Church with more insistence than she uses with regard to devotions in general.

The grant of indulgences — that is, of the remission of temporal punishment still remaining due for sins already forgiven — is an integral part of the power of the keys exercised by the Church in absolution from sin. Indulgences complete the work begun by the sacrament of penance. The sinner has been reconciled with God, but the demands of Divine Justice have still to be satisfied by temporary suffering, endured either on earth or in purgatory. In holy indulgences we have a means of satisfying these demands in an easier way; or, rather, in them the Church has an authoritatively ordained means of making that satisfaction for us — a means purchased, like pardon itself, by the merits of the blood of Jesus Christ. The utility of indulgences, and the power of the Church to grant them, are truths of faith that no Catholic may deny. No one, however, is *bound* to avail himself of them. Nevertheless, it will easily be seen that the rejection of so great a spiritual advantage would argue a still greater want of conformity with the spirit of Catholicism than the rejection of even the most widespread of the devotional practices of which I have hitherto spoken.

The same may be said of the sacramentals. Partly by virtue of the official prayers and blessings of God's representative, the Church, and partly by reason of the faith and devotion of those who use them, sacramentals are true means of grace and are, as such, brought prominently before her children by the Catholic Church. They are closely connected with the sacraments, inasmuch as, by remitting venial sin, they prepare the soul for their worthier reception and because some of them are invariably connected by the Church in her liturgy with the administration of certain sacraments and the celebration of Holy Mass. Thus, the blessing and use of holy water, palms, ashes and candles, and the holy oils find a place in the most solemn liturgical functions. Here again, although there is no compulsion to use these things — except when, as in the case of the holy oils, for instance, they form part of a sacramental rite — a Catholic who should withdraw himself from the universal practice of the Church at large would rightly be suspected of some want of harmony with her spirit.

But beyond indulgences and sacramentals, beyond those devotional practices whose universality is a recommendation not lightly to be passed over, there remain a multitude of devotions that will be useful to some, but by no means to all. These a Catholic may leave aside without the slightest imputation upon his conformity to the mind of the Church. Indeed, to leave them aside may often be a virtue; for it is not to be denied that some, oblivious of the real object of such things — to minister, that is, to the needs of particular souls and to help them forward in the practical life of a Christian — make of the means the end, and turn devotion into a kind of spiritual amusement, to the immense detriment of solid virtue and real progress. This is the fault neither of the devotions, which are excellent in themselves if wisely chosen and properly used, nor of the Church, which approves of them precisely on the understanding that such wise selection and prudent use of them shall be made. It is the fault of the persons who misuse a good thing.

Conclusion

It should be clear, from what has been said in the present chapter, that no one who submits to the Catholic Church will be called upon to take up any special form of devotion as a compulsory duty. The sacraments, Holy Mass, and the commandments of the Church will certainly be imposed upon him as conditions of membership. In all other things he will be free. Since, presumably, by the time he comes to be received into the Church, he will to some extent understand and appreciate her spirit, far from feeling any difficulty in availing himself of the rich treasure of approved devotional practices that she offers to him, and that he is free to take or to leave, he will thank God that he has found the religion that was made to meet every need of every soul; and he will have no hesitation in drawing from that treasury those things that he finds most helpful to the new spiritual life he will have received.

Having made his act of faith, having taken the great venture, he will find that the shadows have fled away and that the bright light of the truth of God illumines his soul. In the great brotherhood of the Catholic Church he will learn to exercise toward the devotional practices of others the respect that Christian charity, as well as the approval of the Church, demands from him and that he, in turn, will receive from his brethren in the Faith. He will see things in their due proportion, as they can be seen only from within; and he will find that his old fears and difficulties about such nonessential matters as it has been my humble endeavor to discuss in these chapters were the creations of misunderstanding and prejudice alone.

Bibliography

"The Church and Liberal Catholicism: Pastoral of the English Bishops." *Messenger of the Sacred Heart* (1901): 180-193.

Franzelin, Johannes Baptist. *Tractatus de Divina Traditione et Scriptura*. Roma: Typographia Polyglotta, 1896.

Joly, Henri, and George Tyrrell. *The Psychology of the Saints*. London, Duckworth, 1898.

Petre, Maude Dominica. *Where Saints Have Trod: Some Studies in Asceticism*. London: Catholic Truth Society, 1903.

Tanner, Norman P. *Decrees of the Ecumenical Councils*. 2 vols. London: Sheed and Ward, 1990.

Thurston, Herbert. *The Holy Year of Jubilee: An Account of the History and Ceremonial of the Roman Jubilee.* London: Sands, 1900.

Sophia Institute

Sophia Institute is a nonprofit institution that seeks to nurture the spiritual, moral, and cultural life of souls and to spread the Gospel of Christ in conformity with the authentic teachings of the Roman Catholic Church.

Sophia Institute Press fulfills this mission by offering translations, reprints, and new publications that afford readers a rich source of the enduring wisdom of mankind.

Sophia Institute also operates two popular online Catholic resources: CrisisMagazine.com and CatholicExchange.com.

Crisis Magazine provides insightful cultural analysis that arms readers with the arguments necessary for navigating the ideological and theological minefields of the day. *Catholic Exchange* provides world news from a Catholic perspective as well as daily devotionals and articles that will help you to grow in holiness and live a life consistent with the teachings of the Church.

In 2013, Sophia Institute launched Sophia Institute for Teachers to renew and rebuild Catholic culture through service to Catholic education. With the goal of nurturing the spiritual, moral, and cultural life of souls, and an abiding respect for the role and work of teachers, we strive to provide materials and programs that are at once enlightening to the mind and ennobling to the heart; faithful and complete, as well as useful and practical.

Sophia Institute gratefully recognizes the Solidarity Association for preserving and encouraging the growth of our apostolate over the course of many years. Without their generous and timely support, this book would not be in your hands.

www.SophiaInstitute.com
www.CatholicExchange.com
www.CrisisMagazine.com
www.SophiaInstituteforTeachers.org

Sophia Institute Press® is a registered trademark of Sophia Institute.
Sophia Institute is a tax-exempt institution as defined by the Internal Revenue Code, Section 501(c)(3). Tax I.D. 22-2548708.